Education

Katie Duckworth

EVANS BROTHERS LIMITED

 Save the Children

Published by Evans Brothers Limited in association with Save the Children UK.

© 2004 Evans Brothers Ltd and the Save the Children Fund

Evans Brothers Limited.
2A Portman Mansions
Chiltern Street
London W1U 6NR

First published 2004

British Library Cataloguing in
Publication Data
Duckworth, Katie
    Education. - (Children's rights)
    1. Right to education - Juvenile literature
    2. Children's rights - Juvenile literature
    I. Title
    323.3'52

ISBN 0 237 52549 6

Printed in China

Credits
Series editor: Louise John
Editor: Nicola Edwards
Designer: Simon Borrough
Production: Jenny Mulvanny

Acknowledgements
Cover: Peter Barker/Save the Children UK
Title page and ends: Peter Barker/Save the Children UK
p6: Caroline Penn
p7: Paul Smith
p8: Neil Cooper
p9: Jodi Bieber/Network
p10: Michael Amendolia/Network
p11a: Michael Amendolia/Network
p11b: Michael Amendolia/Network
p12: Dan White
p13: Dario Mitidieri
p14: Dario Mitidieri
p15a: Dario Mitidieri
p15b: Dario Mitidieri
p16: Tim Hetherington/Network
p17a: Jenny Matthews
p17b: Liba Taylor/Save the Children UK
p18: Kalpesh Lathigra
p19: Kalpesh Lathigra
p20: Neil Cooper
p21: Jenny Matthews
p22: Tim Hetherington/Network
p23a: Tim Hetherington/Network
p23b: Tim Hetherington/Network
p24: Dan White
p25: Liba Taylor/Save the Children UK
p26: John-Pierre Joyce/Save the Children UK
p27a: John-Pierre Joyce/Save the Children UK
p27b: James Brabazon

Contents

All children have rights

The history of rights for children

In 1919 a remarkable British woman called Eglantyne Jebb founded the Save the Children Fund. She wanted to help children who were dying of hunger as a result of the First World War. Four years later, she wrote a special set of statements, a list of children's rights. Eglantyne Jebb said that her aim was "to claim certain rights for children and labour for their universal recognition". This meant that she wanted worldwide agreement on children's rights.

It was many years before countries around the world agreed that children have rights, but eventually the statements became recognised in international law in 1989. They are known as the United Nations Convention on the Rights of the Child (UNCRC). The rights in the UNCRC are based on the idea that everyone deserves fair treatment.

The UNCRC is a very important document. Almost every country in the world has signed it, so it relates to most of the world's children. The rights listed in the UNCRC cover all areas of children's lives such as their right to have a home and their right to be educated.

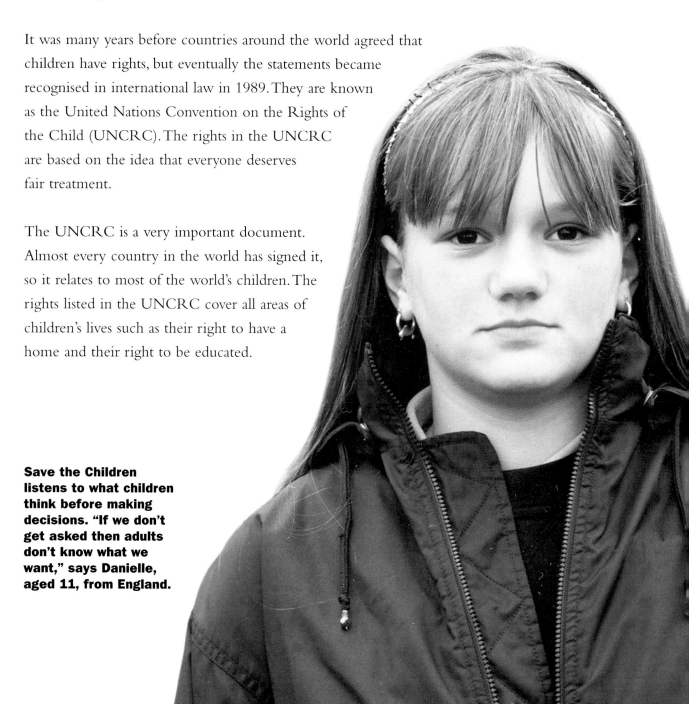

Save the Children listens to what children think before making decisions. "If we don't get asked then adults don't know what we want," says Danielle, aged 11, from England.

Rights for all? The UNCRC should mean that the rights of children everywhere are guaranteed. However, this is not the case. Every day, millions of children are denied their rights. Children in many countries suffer discrimination because they are poor, or disabled, or because they work for a living. It might be because of their religion, race or whether they are a boy or a girl.

Children are very vulnerable, so they need special care and protection. The UNCRC exists to try to make sure that they are cared for and protected.

The right to an education Some of the Articles in the UNCRC are about every child's right to an education. With a good education, children can have more opportunities and make choices about their lives. Here are some of the Articles:

Article 28 You have the right to an education.

Article 29 You have the right to an education which tries to develop your personality and abilities as much as possible and encourages you to respect other people's rights and values and to respect the environment.

Children, like these boys in Colombia, have the right to a good education so they can get the best start in life.

Article 42 You have the right to learn about your rights.

Save the Children Save the Children UK is part of the International Save the Children Alliance, working in over 100 countries worldwide to make children's rights a reality. This book and the others in the series tell the stories of children around the world who are achieving their rights with the help of Save the Children projects.

Children who are poor have the right to an education

Missing school   Every day throughout the world, more than 110 million children miss out on going to primary school. This means that these children may never learn to read and write.

One reason children cannot go to school is because their families do not have enough money. In some developing countries parents have to pay for their children's education. Sometimes, as well as school fees, parents also have to find the money for uniforms, pens and books.

Education gives children the chance to build a better future for themselves and their families.

Children who work   Children who are poor often do not go to school because they go out to work instead. In some countries, even very young children have jobs to help their families make ends meet. You can find out more about working children on page 12.

The right to go to school   All children, rich or poor, have the right to go to school. Education is as important as the right to food and a home. Education offers children the chance to escape from poverty. It opens

"Education is the way out of poverty."

Nyarai, 16, Zimbabwe

doors to better-paid, more interesting jobs and gives people the confidence to believe that there is a lot they can achieve.

Education is priceless

Almost everywhere in the world education is highly valued. Many poor families make a real effort to make sure their children go to school. Parents or grandparents try to save money for fees and go without food and new clothes. Children who live in the countryside, like Nhung (see pages 10 and 11), often have to walk miles to school if there is no bus or they cannot afford the fare.

The right to a good education

Children have a right, not just to an education, but to a good education. Some schools in poor countries are hardly worth going to. There are not enough teachers and pupils may have to share desks or even chairs. In Tanzania, in Africa, there are sometimes 75 children in a class and 20 children may have to share a single textbook. Many families prefer their children, especially the girls, to stay at home instead, and help out.

To have a good education, children need to be taught by well-trained teachers who respect and value their pupils. All children should be given the chance to develop the skills and talents that will be useful to them in the future.

Nhung's story

It was five o'clock in the morning in the village of Dong Moc in Vietnam. The sun's rays were just creeping over the mountain tops when ten-year-old Nhung gave a noisy yawn, stretched and clambered out of her warm bed. Her body was still sleepy but it was time to get up.

She could hear the chickens and ducks scuttling about in the yard. Nhung flung on her clothes and tiptoed across the kitchen where she carefully picked up the feeding bucket so it didn't clatter and wake everyone up. As she scattered the rice she tried to count the feathery bodies pecking away. Six, seven, eight, nine. Or had she counted that one already? It was confusing now that so many new ducklings and chicks had been born.

The air was so cold that her breath puffed out like white smoke. She dashed back inside and very soon Nhung and her brother were ready to serve the family breakfast – rice soup. Nhung would love to have chopped up some tasty chicken for it, or even some vegetables. But there was nothing. Her mum and dad did not have the money for treats.

Nhung's mother is wearing a traditional Dao outfit. Children from this ethnic group are usually too poor to go to school.

Nhung didn't mind – as long as she could go to school. Many poor families in the village did not send their children to school at all because they didn't have the money for books and pens. She knew she was lucky.

Going to school means a lot to Nhung. "I feel happy in the mornings when I think about going there," she says.

Nhung loved everything about school. She enjoyed the walk there, playing and chatting with her friends. She liked speaking in Vietnamese, a different language from the Dao she spoke at home. She loved learning to count, too.

Save the Children works in several schools like Nhung's, training teachers and helping children to learn to speak Vietnamese, the language in which the lessons are taught.

Being able to go to school has made a big difference to Nhung. Just yesterday she had read all the way through a family wedding invitation without stumbling. Her mum and dad had never learned to read and write, but now Nhung could. It made her so proud.

Nhung is doing well at primary school but she may not be able to go on to secondary level. It will cost her parents £50 a year.

Children who work have the right to an education

> **"I don't think that children should work. They should get an education instead."**
>
> Guddi, 16, India

These working children from Cambodia have a right to be at school.

Working for a living Around the world, there are about 350 million children who work and half of them work in dangerous jobs. Children do all sorts of jobs, often for nothing or just a few pence. Some are servants in other people's homes, working long hours cooking and cleaning. Other children sell vegetables or shine shoes in markets or on the street. Sometimes they work in dangerous and dirty factories, workshops or mines. Working children usually have no time to go to school or they are just too tired to learn.

Why children work

In many poor countries, some children miss school because they have to help their families with farming or housework. Boys and girls tend to do different kinds of work. Children also work in family businesses or have evening jobs to increase the household income.

Most children go out to work because their families need their wages. Others have nobody to look after them, so they have to work to earn money to survive.

Working children's rights

Some families are so poor that everyone has to contribute, but work should be safe and not interfere with children's education. Even if they are working, children have a right to go to school.

They need schools that suit them. This might mean that classes are held at weekends and teachers are employed who understand which subjects are most useful to working children.

As well as being taught how to read and write, pupils learn how to run their businesses better or to avoid exploitation by employers. Guddi works in a factory in India, making glass bangles. At her school for working children she is learning new skills like reading and maths to help her get a better job when she is older.

Guddi would like to help others escape from poverty through education. Going to school means working children like her can become more confident and learn how to stand up for their rights.

Children who have had an education are more able to help others when they have grown up, perhaps by becoming teachers themselves.

Nancy's story

Nancy put the last tiny stitch into the brightly-coloured wall hanging. She eased herself up from the floor to stretch her aching back. Her fingers were stinging from where she had pricked herself with the needle and her head throbbed after the long day's work. But at least there would be two pieces of embroidery to sell today. Her mum and dad really needed what she could earn.

Just then the door flew open and her after-work club teacher rushed in. A giant stack of books wobbled under her arm. "Good evening," she announced, handing out the books. "It is time for your lesson."

Soon the chatter of Nancy and her five workmates filled the room. Nancy's head was quickly buzzing with the day's lesson. Today it was division. She was proud of her progress with numbers. It made it easier to calculate how much to charge for her embroidery. Too soon her teacher said goodbye and it was time for evening prayers.

Nancy at home in Kashmir.

Outside the sun had sunk out of sight behind Lake Dal, close to where Nancy lived in Kashmir. Nancy wandered back to her house, her head full of thoughts. If only she could go to school full time. If only she never had to embroider another stitch. If only she could fulfil her dream and become a doctor. For a moment, life felt very unfair.

"Nancy! Nancy!" Her father was calling her. He worked as a boatman, ferrying people across the lake. She ran to join him as he tied up his worn out boat. "Not so good again today," he said, shaking his head. "Never mind. Tomorrow will be better." Nancy smiled. Her dad was always so

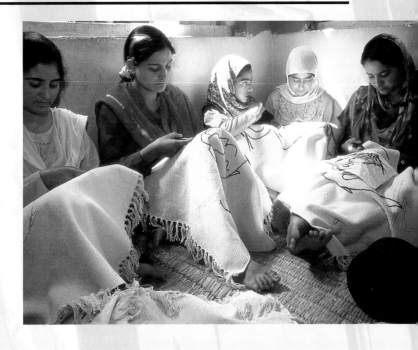

Nancy has a job embroidering patterns on to wall hangings. "I started doing this work when I was six," she says. "I have to work for my family."

hopeful about the future. How could she even think about not working? At least she had the after-work club to look forward to. She felt proud that her embroidery was helping to pay for her younger sister's schooling.

Nancy's club was set up by Save the Children. There, working children learn how to read and write and do accounts. It helps them to avoid being cheated by the middlemen who buy their work and then sell it to shops at a higher price.

15

Children who are disabled have the right to an education

Equal rights Disabled children want and need the same things as non-disabled children: love, friends, food, fun and a home. Most also want to go to school. Children with mental and physical disabilities have a right to a good education, but it is not always easy for them to get one.

Disabled children Children from poor families sometimes miss out on education completely. In fact, only a tiny number of disabled children in developing countries go to school. There are several reasons for this. Some families are ashamed of their disabled child so they hide him or her away at home. It also costs money to go to school, so if parents have to make difficult choices about which of their children to send, their disabled child is usually last on the list. It is not fair, but it happens a lot.

Prejudice A big problem for disabled children is the prejudice of other people. Disabled children sometimes do not enjoy school because other children tease and bully them. This is often because it is easy to pick on children who are 'different' in some way. It can leave children with disabilities feeling sad and lonely, but it can often make them very brave and determined, like Narayan. You can read Narayan's story on pages 18 and 19.

Mbowa goes to school in the Democratic Republic of Congo. In some developing countries, only two out of every hundred children who are disabled go to school.

"It's good to be with the other children because they can play with us and understand us."

Mbowa, 14, Democratic Republic of Congo

Children's needs

It does not have to be difficult or expensive to give disabled children a good education. Teachers, families and other people in the neighbourhood should try to understand what different children need. The best way to do this is to listen to what they want. For example, Mbowa, who is physically disabled, goes to a school where there are disabled and non-disabled children. Most disabled children say this is the sort of school they want.

Many children with disabilities need practical help to get the most out of their education. They might need to sit at the front of the class, or use equipment. Having a 'buddy' to look out for them is a great way to help a disabled pupil to feel included. A buddy might help with eating lunch, getting to the toilet or writing notes for a deaf child in class.

James has a disability. He has the right to go to school so that he can get the most out of life.

Braille equipment means this Ethiopian girl can join in lessons with her non-disabled classmates.

Narayan's story

Narayan is 16 and lives in a village in the Himalayas in Nepal. When he was little, he had a disease called polio which damaged his legs, so he cannot walk easily. Even though he is disabled he thinks of himself as very lucky. He goes to school and is surrounded by caring friends and teachers.

When Narayan was very young he used to crawl about on his hands and knees. He even crawled to school along mountain paths. The other children were cruel to him because they thought he was different. They bullied him and called him monkey. "I'd stay silent," he says, "but inside I felt unhappy."

Narayan has become more confident since becoming a member of his local children's group. He has spoken out in his community about disabled children's rights.

Narayan's family encouraged him to go to school even though he is disabled. "They haven't treated me any differently because of my disability," he says.

To help him out, Narayan's brothers made him walking sticks from branches. They kept getting broken but after years of practice, by the time Narayan was 14, he had taught himself to walk. Now he walks everywhere and keeps his muscles strong by doing exercises every day.

Narayan belongs to a children's group supported by Save the Children that runs a campaign for disabled children to go to school. He walks from house to house in his village chatting to parents about why they should send their disabled children to school. He gets very excited when he succeeds in persuading a hesitant mum or dad.

Narayan enjoys going to school. He has lots of friends to help him carry his books, and other children do not bully him anymore. They have learned that disabled children need friends too.

Of course, Narayan complains about school sometimes. On some days there are 100 students in his classroom. It is hot and crowded and Narayan says there is hardly space to open their books, but he is happy to be there. Narayan's dream is to teach children in the future and he knows he needs an education to make his dream come true.

Children who are homeless have the right to an education

Homeless children need to learn that using clean water will help them to stay healthy.

Street children For some children, home is the street. Street children are very unlikely to be given an education. Because their parents are too poor to care for them or because they do not get on well with their families, these children may have made their way to cities to earn a living. Street children work hard, so there is little time to play or go to school.

Children living on the street deserve a proper education. They are more likely to escape from poverty if they can read and write. Street life can be dangerous, so it's important that the children learn how to take care of themselves.

In some cities, such as Kinshasa in the Democratic Republic of Congo, where there are many street children, clubs and schools have been set up to provide them with an education. You can read Jimmy's story on page 22.

Disasters Children who have had to leave home suddenly because of disasters or war find their right to an education may be denied too. Families may have to abandon their homes and go to live in temporary camps. It is not easy to carry on an education in a camp. There may be no school at all or it may be crowded, without blackboards, chairs or books. Also, when children are feeling shocked and upset, it is difficult for them to learn easily.

But it's important for children to receive an education, even if they are away from home for a short time. Lessons help them make friends and feel settled. Education also allows them to fit back more easily into normal life when the disaster or war is over and they can go home. You can read more about education during disasters on pages 24 and 25.

These Palestinian girls enjoy doing their homework together in the refugee camp where they live.

Jimmy's story

Jimmy is probably 13 years old. That might seem a strange thing to say, but he is not quite sure when he was born.

Something he is sure about is that he would like to go to school. But instead, Jimmy spends his days pacing the hot, dusty streets of Kinshasa, the capital of the Democratic Republic of Congo. He doesn't have time to go to school, and, anyway, school is too expensive. Jimmy only earns 80 pence a day selling water and doing odd jobs.

His life was not always so difficult. When he was little, Jimmy lived happily with his family. His mum and dad cared for him and he enjoyed playing with his five brothers and sisters. One of the best things about being at home was that he went to school.

Jimmy's childhood seems a long time ago now. He had just started primary school when his mum died. His dad could not cope with all the children so Jimmy was sent to live with his aunt and then his grandma. His big brother beat him and stopped him from playing with his friends, so Jimmy decided to run away.

It was a scary time for a little boy alone on the streets. Soon he made friends with some other street children and found a floor to sleep on in a centre run by the church. Now he sells drinking

Jimmy has a right to an education. He lives and works on the streets of a big city.

22

water with other boys. In the evening, they share what they have earned. If they make a lot of money they celebrate by buying new clothes or eating a big meal together.

Jimmy goes to a special club for street children. They talk about their problems and find ways of looking after themselves on the dangerous streets. But what Jimmy really wants is a proper home and to go to school. When he was little he dreamed of being a government minister. Now he would like to be a car mechanic, but he knows he has to go to school first.

"If my mother and father were around, you'd never see me here on the streets. I'd be in school," says Jimmy.

Homeless children, like Jimmy and his friends, need a safe place to relax, play and learn.

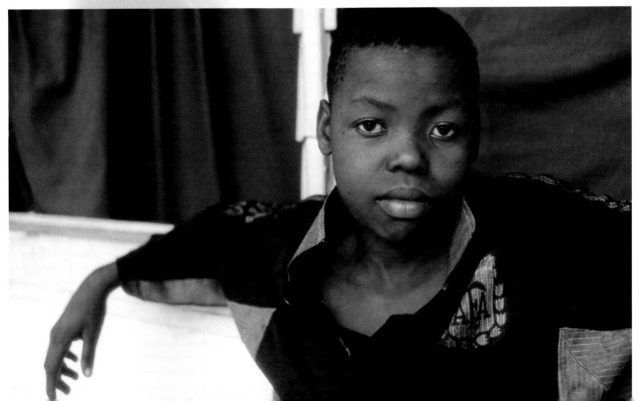

Children caught up in an emergency have the right to an education

The world turned upside-down An emergency is a major disaster. The lives of people caught up in disasters are changed dramatically, often in an instant. Disasters such as earthquakes and floods can destroy buildings like schools and homes in no time at all. War is an emergency, too.

The effect on children Have you ever seen news reports on television about a disaster, such as a famine? Perhaps your school collected money to help. You might imagine that people in emergencies just want somewhere safe to live and food to eat, but children should still have their rights protected, including the right to an education. Sadly, in an emergency, children often miss out on going to school.

It's good to learn It is really important that children continue to learn in emergency situations. Going to school helps children cope better with the disruption to their normal life. They keep up with their studies and can be with their friends.

After an emergency, children look forward to returning to their lessons, but there may no longer be a school to go to.

The right education It is not easy to learn when your world has been turned upside-down. Children may be shocked and upset. People they love may be missing or dead. In these situations, children need a special kind of education. Teachers and carers should be trained to listen and to allow children to take part in decisions about their education.

Children in emergency situations may study different subjects to the ones you learn at school. In a drought, they learn how to protect the environment. Children who live in countries torn apart by conflict learn about getting on with others, so that they can contribute to a peaceful future.

Refugees People who flee to find safety in other countries are called refugees. More than half the world's refugees are under the age of 18. Refugee children have the right to an education. Even in the UK, refugees don't always get as good an education as other children, but they should. There may be children who are refugees in your class. Think about what you could do to make them feel at home.

HIV and AIDS The HIV virus attacks the body and makes it unable to fight off any disease. HIV then develops into AIDS. HIV is spread when blood or other bodily fluids from an infected person mix with another person's. The spread of the HIV virus is a special kind of emergency because so many people in so many countries are affected by it. Children have a right to learn about HIV and AIDS, so that they know how to protect themselves. There is no cure for AIDS, so avoiding it is very important.

DID YOU KNOW?
Every minute of the day, a child dies of AIDS.

Children's clubs give their members information which helps them to protect themselves against HIV/AIDS. "I think it's a good idea to tell children about AIDS because they can tell other children about it," says Liberia, aged 11, from Uganda.

Flamur and Betim's stories

Betim and Flamur live in Kosovo in Eastern Europe. In 1999, Serbian soldiers began to attack and burn villages there. Both boys suddenly had to flee from their homes because their families no longer felt safe. Betim and Flamur were sad to leave behind their friends, favourite toys, and their much-loved schools.

Flamur   Flamur was eight years old when his family had to escape by train to a refugee camp in the former Yugoslav Republic of Macedonia. Flamur remembers some good things about living there but he was anxious about his grandma who had stayed behind. Like Betim, he missed his friends and his school. He was safe, but really he wanted to go home.

The camp where he lived was well organised. There was a special Save the Children centre where separated children and parents could be reunited, and a school had been set up. Here Flamur could play in the children's play area and carry on with his reading and writing. But it wasn't the same as being at home. Flamur didn't really feel like playing and learning without his friends.

Flamur is much happier now that he is home again.

26

Betim Betim was 12 when he had to flee his homeland - twice. The first time his family escaped, relatives in the capital city invited them to stay. It was much safer here away from the bombs and bullets, but Betim was lonely. The local children welcomed him but inside he felt he did not belong. All he could think about was his own school. Would it still be standing when he returned? Would there be any teachers?

Emergency food is distributed to people in Kosovo who had left their homes because of fighting.

After two months his family was able to go home. As the bus drew into his village he was so excited he did not know where to go first, his home or his school. His heart was pounding as he went in search of his school. It was still there!

Betim was overjoyed to be back but then the violence started all over again. The family had to move out of their home again. This time they camped in the nearby woods. Betim really wanted to go to school, but there wasn't one.

At last, the soldiers left his village. As soon as they heard it was safe, Betim and his family rushed home. This time he was not so lucky. His school was a pile of rubble.

Betim and his friends had lessons in tents while their school was being rebuilt. Now they have a brand-new school. Betim is studying hard and thinking of becoming a lawyer.

During the war, Betim was desperate to get back to his school. "I thought that even if all the village was burned I just didn't want my school to be burned."

27

Glossary

AIDS Acquired Immune Deficiency Syndrome: AIDS is caused by a virus which attacks the body's immune system and makes it unable to fight off any disease.

article A part of a legal document, such as a convention.

children's rights The rights that everyone under the age of 18 should have, including the right to life, the right to food, clothes and a place to live, the right to education and health, and the right to be protected from danger.

conflict A serious disagreement between two or more groups of people which can lead to fighting.

developing countries Countries which have few industries and in which many people are very poor.

disabled When part of the body does not work properly. Sometimes children are born with a disability or it may be the result of an accident. Disabilities can be physical (to do with the body) or mental (to do with the mind).

discrimination The unfair treatment of a person because of their race, religion or whether they are a boy or a girl.

drought A long period with little or no rainfall, when people cannot get enough water to drink or water their crops.

ethnic group A group of people who share the same race and language.

exploitation Unfairly taking advantage of a person, for example, if an employer pays children very little for working long hours in a factory.

famine A severe shortage of food, when people cannot get enough to eat because they have no food crops or they cannot buy food. People may die of starvation during a famine.

founded A word meaning started.

HIV Human Immunodeficiency Virus: the virus that leads to AIDS.

non-disabled When the body works properly.

polio An infectious disease that is caused by a virus. Polio affects the brain and muscles of the body and can cause paralysis.

poverty A lack of money which results in a poor standard of living.

prejudice A negative opinion of someone based on looks, behaviour, race, religion etc rather than on fact.

projects Schemes that are set up to improve life for local people.

refugee camp A place where people who have had to leave their homes can live, usually for a short time, until it is safe for them to return.

refugees People who leave their home country because they feel unsafe.

street children Children who are homeless and live on the streets of a city rather than with their families.

United Nations An organisation made up of many different countries which was set up in 1945 to promote international peace and cooperation.

Index

Further reading and addresses

Books to read

Save the Children (*Taking Action* series), Heinemann Library/
Save the Children, 2000

Stand Up, Speak Out, Two-Can Publishing, 2001

Packs for teachers

Partners in Rights (a photo pack using creative arts to explore
rights and citizenship for 7-14 year olds), Save the Children,
2000

A Time for Rights (explores citizenship and rights in relation to
the UN Convention on the Rights of the Child, for 9-13 year
olds), Save the Children/UNICEF 2002

Young Citizens (a pack looking at the lives of five young citizens
around the world, for Key Stage 2), Save the Children, 2002

There is a summary version of the UN Convention on the
Rights of the Child at www.childrensrights.ie/yourrights.php

Useful addresses

Save the Children
1 St John's Lane
London EC1
www.savethechildren.org.uk

UNICEF UK
Africa House
64-78 Kingsway
London WC2B 6NB
www.unicef.org

Save the Children Australia
Level 3
20 Council St
Hawthorn East
Vic 3123
www.savethechildren.org.au

UNICEF Australia
Level 3
303 Pitt St
Sydney
NSW 2000
www.unicef.com.au